Sorbets and Ice Creams

Sorbets and

Ice Creams

& Other Frozen Confections

Lou Seibert Pappas

Photographs by

Frankie Frankeny

CHRONICLE BOOKS

SAN FRANCISCO

Library of Congress Cataloging-in-Publication Data:

Pappas, Lou Seibert.

  Sorbets and ice creams & other frozen confections /

  by Lou Seibert Pappas: photographs by Frankie Frankeny.

                    p.   cm.

   Includes index.

   ISBN 0-8118-1573-0

   1. Ice cream, ices, etc. 2. Frozen desserts. I. Title.

TX795.P28 1997

641.8'62—dc20   96-28040

                                            CIP

Printed in Hong Kong.

Design and illustrations by Brenda Rae Eno

Food Styling by Elizabeth Falkner and Frankie Frankeny.

Prop Styling by Kelly and Frankie Frankeny.

The photographer wishes to thank Laurel Corkran, Sarah Bolles, Martine Trélaün, Brenda Rae Eno, and St. Francis Fountain.

Distributed in Canada by Raincoast Books

8680 Cambie Street

Vancouver, B.C. V6P 6M9

10 9 8 7 6 5 4 3 2 1

Chronicle Books

85 Second Street

San Francisco, CA 94105

Web Site: www. chronbooks.com

Acknowledgments

With special thanks to Paulette Fono, Betsy Fryberger, Tita Kolozsi, Cindy Race, and Dina Viggiano, and my many friends who indulged in the Sunday tasting parties. Again, Carolyn Miller proved an invaluable editor.

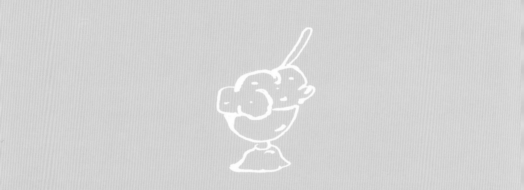

Contents

Introduction

CHURNING HOMEMADE ICE CREAM was a Sunday ritual when I was a child growing up in Oregon's verdant Willamette Valley. Daddy would pick up a big ice block from the local creamery, chop it in a gunny sack, and Mother would prepare the custard mix. The big Hobart electric mixer would hum and whirl up a half-gallon of ice cream in vanilla, three-fruit, peppermint stick, or strawberry flavor. My sister and brother and I vied to lick the luscious creaminess from the blades of the dasher.

At the small seaside resort of Neskowin every summer, the big daily treat was indulging in a chocolate-covered, almond-coated ice cream bar made nearby at the Tillamook Creamery. For a nickel a scoop in the 1940s, my friends and I consumed a trio of ice cream scoops from my hometown's college creamery in Corvallis, Oregon.

Later, raising a family in California, I attached a wooden bucket to my Kitchen Aid mixer, packed it with ice and rock salt, and turned out myriad new flavors in the tin canister. A neighbor with a cow in rural Portola Valley gave us gallons of cream weekly, so I could re-create the exquisite flavors we had sampled on European trips.

On an Italian sojourn in the sixties, I discovered gelato, semifreddo, and festive frozen bombes. On successive trips I learned more about these delectable frozen sweets and returned to reproduce them for *Sunset* magazine stories.

My Greek father-in-law shared his secret for making a proper ice cream soda for our four children. And he knew. He opened his first ice cream parlor in San Francisco in 1905, the year before the Great Earthquake, and installed one of the first modern soda fountains on the Pacific Coast at his ice cream–candy store, Elite Confections, at Fifth and Market streets. He offered strawberry, vanilla, chocolate, maple nut, and coffee flavors, along with high-grade candies. A faded sepia photograph shows Papa in the candy jar–filled shop, standing alongside a little boy wearing knickers and a cap and licking an ice cream cone.

I have savored sublime ices and ice cream on food trips all over the world. Frozen desserts, then as now, are my passion. While my companions ordered chocolate tortes and pastries, I chose sorbet plates and parfaits.

The ice cream in Scandinavia was some of the best, made with ultra-rich cream and embellished with berries, bittersweet chocolate, almond praline, and whipped cream, and served in goblets and just-baked sugar cones.

France offered exquisite fruit sorbets served in tuile cookies with exotic fruits and swirls of raspberry coulis on porcelain dessert plates. In Paris I would make a beeline to Berthillon on the Île St-Louis, and join a queue of French schoolchildren to choose *pistache*, *framboise*, and *café* from among two dozen sorbets and *glaces*. There at 31, rue St-Louis-en-l'Île, I enjoyed delicious perfection.

I have savored dazzling creations at Michelin-starred restaurants: pear sorbet and strawberry and vanilla bean *glace* at Gérard Boyer's Les Crayères in Reims; licorice *glace* at Marc Meneau's L'Esperance in St-Père-sous-Vézelay and a stellar pineapple ice at Joel Robuchon's Jamin in Paris. At the Lenôtre shops in Paris, the fluted papers of little individual *glaces* of *café*, *framboise*, *noisettes*, and *citron* are almost too perfect to consume.

At Perchè No? in Florence, I ecstatically ate *gelati* in such flavors as zabaglione, Grand Marnier, and rum raisin. *Tartufo*, *gianduia*, and *nocciola* were other tantalizing delights.

Memorable American ice cream specialties include Amaretto ice cream in a boat-shaped filo crust at Mary Elaine's in Scottsdale; a pine nut caramel ice cream at the Inn of the Anasazi in Santa Fe, and an elegant honey ice cream with blueberries at Domaine Chandon in the Napa Valley.

Ice cream and carts have turned up at unexpected places in my travels. A peach ice was heavenly after a tour of the Turkish ruins of Ephesus. Ginger ice cream was a treat on the streets of Amsterdam; and a cassis and gingerbread ice cream was a delightful surprise at a Munich beer hall. Passion fruit–guava sherbet became a favorite Hawaiian memory; rum ice cream in a pineapple shell was the highlight of a Malaysian banana plantation; mango sorbet with tropical fruits starred in South Africa; and garlic ice cream was a unique experience at the Gilroy Garlic Festival.

With today's frozen-cylinder ice cream freezers, ice creams and sorbets like the ones in this book can be everyday delights in your own kitchen.

History

THE CHINESE PRACTICED the art of making iced drinks and desserts as long ago as 1100 B.C. by running water mixed with saltpeter over containers filled with fruit juice and honey. The Arabs followed, making syrups chilled with snow, called *sharbets*, the forerunners of sherbet and sorbet.

During the rule of Nero in A.D. 54–68, he sent runners into the mountains for snow, which was relayed back to his table and flavored with honey, juices, and wine. In the thirteenth century, Marco Polo brought back to Venice the Chinese secret of cooling liquid without ice. Thus the great fashion for ices began in Italy.

When Catherine de Médicis arrived in France in 1533 to marry the future Henri II, she introduced iced desserts to the court. More than a century later, in 1670, Procopio Coltelli, a Sicilian, opened a cafe in Paris that served sorbets. Café Procope is still in operation today. During the next century, a succession of Parisian cafes introduced ice cream specialties. From the Café Napolitain on the Boulevard des Italiens, for example, came Biscuit Tortoni, the macaroon, rum, and ice cream concoction named for the café's Italian proprietor. In England in 1747, Hannah Glasse published the *The Art of Cookery Made Easy*, which included ice cream recipes.

But it was America that really pioneered the refinement of ice cream. George Washington had an ice machine, and Thomas Jefferson served baked Alaska. Dolly Madison glamorized ice cream by serving it at White House state dinners. In 1777, the first ads for ice cream appeared in the New York *Post Boy*. The hand-cranked freezer was invented in 1846 by Nancy Johnson, and in 1851 ice cream began to be made on a commercial scale. *Godey's Lady's Book* claimed that ice cream had become one of the necessities of life in the 1850s.

New Yorker Italo Marchiony created the first ice cream cone in 1896 and was granted a 1903 patent. The cone was reinvented a year later by a waffle maker at the St. Louis Exposition, when an ice cream vendor at a nearby stand ran out of dishes and had to find a substitute. It was an instant hit, and before long, St. Louis founderies were banging out molds for what was then called the World's Fair Cornucopia. Three frozen novelties—the Eskimo Pie, the Good Humor Bar, and the Popsicle—were launched a few years later in the 1920s and remain popular today.

Hollywood movies gave a boost to ice cream in the thirties and forties by setting scenes in small-town soda fountains. After a movie, the place to go in that era was a drive-in or an ice cream parlor for a sundae or soda. In the fifties, soda fountains went into decline when packaged ice cream became available in supermarkets. America went for economy, licking mass-produced ice creams that were filled with stabilizers and inflated with air. The past two decades have seen a rediscovery of and a resurging demand for premium ice creams and sorbets, along with frozen yogurt and ice cream novelties. Manufacturers have responded with a wealth of quality products.

Glossary

Bombe: A frozen dessert consisting of layers of ice cream or sherbet, usually formed in a rounded mold.

Gelato (Italian plural *gelati*): Italian ice cream, characterized by intense flavor and often served semi-frozen. In Italy, each cafe often makes its own gelato with fresh fruits and other pure ingredients. The word gelato refers to various styles of ice cream, from light to richer versions.

Glace: The French word for ice cream.

Granita (Italian plural *granite*): A type of Italian ice that is coarse in texture and often less intensely flavored than sorbetto.

Ice: A coarsely textured frozen mixture of water, sugar, and liquid flavoring such as fruit juice, wine, coffee, or tea.

Ice Cream: A frozen confection made from milk and/or cream, sugar or another sweetener, and a flavoring such as chocolate, nuts, fruit, or spices. By FDA standards, it must contain a minimum of 10 percent butterfat (8 percent for some flavors), 16 to 20 percent milk solids, and not more than 50 percent overrun. Premium ice creams and French-style ice creams usually have a cooked egg-custard base.

Parfait: Ice cream layered with flavored syrup or fruit and whipped cream, served in footed parfait glasses.

Semifreddo: An Italian ice cream lightened with whipped cream, custard, or beaten egg yolks or whites and often a sugar syrup. The word means "half frozen."

Sorbet: The French word for sherbet, which is made without milk but is finer in texture and usually more intensely flavored than an ice. Sorbets are usually made from fruit purees, water, and sugar.

Sorbetto (Italian plural *sorbetti*): Italian sherbet.

Basic Techniques and Ingredients

Ice cream and ices can be made in various styles of ice cream makers or in freezer compartments. An ice cream maker is not necessary for ices, granitas, and sorbets. Instead, an electric mixer or food processor provides the essential whipping action once the mixture is first frozen.

The basic categories of ice cream makers include the canister packed with salt and ice in a wooden or plastic bucket, powered by a hand crank or electric motor; the frozen-cylinder maker with a crank that must be rotated by hand every few minutes; the frozen cylinder that is inserted in a base and revolved by an electric motor while the dasher remains stationary; and an ice cream maker with a self-contained refrigeration unit.

The preparation of ice cream involves three stages: preparing the mix, freezing it, and ripening or firming it after the freezing process.

Ice cream is a liquid mixture that is stabilized by freezing much of the liquid. The proportion of the ingredients and the preparation technique determine the quality of the ice cream. Tiny well-dispersed ice crystals create a smooth, creamy product. Large, chunky ice crystals create an unpleasant grainy texture.

Though ice creams, sorbets, ices, and still-frozen desserts are considered to be "frozen," they are not completely so. Instead, tiny ice crystals are suspended in a binding syrup of sugar, with or without fat and/or protein. While much of the water in the mixture freezes, the concentration of sugar and other substances lowers the water's freezing temperature so the dessert will not solidify. Cream, milk, and eggs also work as buffers to separate tiny crystals from one another. Beating air in by churning the mixture in an ice cream maker helps to keep the crystals apart and makes the texture smooth. When ice cream begins to thicken and becomes viscous, it starts to retain air well. Alcohol, honey, and corn syrup lower the freezing point of the mixture, so desserts made with them will usually be softer since a lower percentage of the mixture will freeze solid.

Once the mix has been cooked, it should be refrigerated and cooled to 40°F. Once cream is added, stirring before freezing should be minimal, as the fat particles could turn to flecks of butter. The method of freezing also influences texture. Cooling ice cream rapidly with continuous movement ensures many small crystals with a finer texture, rather than a few larger ones.

If the ice cream maker is the type packed with ice and salt, rock salt is preferred to table salt for several reasons. It is cheaper, it is less likely to sift through the ice and fall to the bottom, and it dissolves more slowly, lowering the temperature more gradually. Too cold a brine will produce a coarse ice cream with too little incorporated air. A good proportion of ice to rock salt is 8 parts ice to 1 part salt.

Ice cream should be made according to the manufacturer's instructions for the ice cream maker. When filling an ice cream maker with an ice cream mixture, allow a head space of at least 2 inches as the mixture will expand during churning as air is whipped in. This aeration, called overrun, or loft, improves the texture of the ice cream and prevents it from becoming a solid block of ice.

Storing Ice Cream

After being frozen in an ice cream maker, ice cream is usually placed in the freezer for 1 hour or longer to firm up, or "ripen." This also allows the flavors to blend. Ideally, ice cream should be stored at fairly low temperatures, between minus 10° and 0°F, to maintain its fine texture and flavor. It should be tightly covered so it doesn't pick up off odors and so that moisture does not settle onto its surface, forming large crystals. A sheet of plastic wrap pressed onto the surface of the ice cream is a good idea.

The gradual coarsening of texture during freezing is due to repeated partial thawings when serving or fluctuations in the temperature of the freezer. Ice crystals grow during storage because whenever ice cream is warmed slightly, the smallest crystals melt. When the temperature drops again, the additional water is taken up by the surviving crystals, which get larger and larger. The lower the average storage temperature of the freezer, the less change takes place.

SERVING ICE CREAM

Ice creams, sorbets, ices, and frozen yogurts should be allowed to warm to about 30°F before serving for best flavor and texture. This allows them to achieve a slightly creamy consistency rather than a solid one. If the ice cream is firmly frozen, transfer it to the refrigerator for 20 to 30 minutes before scooping and serving, but don't let it thaw too much as repeated thawing and refreezing will destroy its texture.

Homemade ices, sorbets, and frozen yogurts are best served within 1 to 2 days, but they may be kept for up to a week or longer. With longer storage, the smooth texture develops larger ice crystals. Ice cream made with a cooked egg custard will keep longer, for several days or a week.

Basic Ingredients

Many commercial ice cream manufacturers use emulsifiers and stabilizers to improve the texture of their ice cream. This is not necessary in homemade ice cream prepared in small quantities with top-quality ingredients.

CREAM: The butterfat in cream is responsible for the rich, smooth texture of ice cream. Using all cream, however, increases the chance of producing ice cream flecked with butter, and too much fat can give the dessert a sticky, heavy texture.

EGGS: Egg yolks act as emulsifiers in a custard base and keep the fat globules from the cream from clumping together.

FRUIT: Most fruits contain pectin and fiber and help keep milk fat and water molecules in an even suspension.

HALF-AND-HALF OR MILK: Milk fat forms small globules and helps keep the water molecules dispersed.

SUGAR: Water in which sugar has dissolved has a freezing point below 32°F. Because of the sugar, not all the water in the mixture freezes and the ice cream does not become solid. Honey or corn syrup produce the same result.

NUTS, CANDIES, AND LIQUEURS: These ingredients add flavor. In churned desserts, nuts and candies are best added when the mixture is partially frozen, and liqueurs should be added when the mixture is almost completely frozen.

Ice Cream Makers

Manufacturers offer ice cream makers to suit every budget. One of the best for the price is KRUPS LA GLACIÈRE, an electric machine with a cylinder container that must be frozen ahead. A compact and stylish design, it produces 1 generous quart of excellent, smooth ice cream in 20 to 25 minutes. Additional cylinders are available separately so that more than one ice cream can be made in a day.

The DONVIER manual model and its clones use a cylinder container that must be frozen ahead. It requires hand cranking every few minutes.

The VITANTONIO GELATO MODO is a manual maker with a cylinder container that must be frozen ahead and hand cranked every 4 to 5 minutes during the freezing time. An electric model is available by the same brand.

WILLIAMS-SONOMA has introduced a top-of-the-line ice cream machine with its own refrigeration unit in a space-efficient model. It makes 1 ½ quarts. After the first batch, the bowl may be removed and a second batch can be churned in the built-in container. It retails for around $400 and is a more affordable compact model than the SIMAC II GELATAIO MAGNUM, a $600 electric machine with self-contained refrigeration.

The RIVAL electric model has a metal canister and a lightweight wooden bucket that uses ice and salt. It comes in a 4-quart capacity.

The traditional WHITE MOUNTAIN hand-cranked wooden ice cream bucket is still available, as it has been for over a century. It is also available in an electric version. Both kinds come in a range of sizes.

Ices, Sorbets, Granitas, and Frozen Yogurts

ULTRA REFRESHING AND light in style, ices, sorbets, and granitas are virtually fat-free. Frozen yogurts are lower in fat as well. These frozen sweets are perfect for many occasions, as mid-afternoon cool refreshments on a summer day to pretty first courses, palate cleansers, or desserts.

Lemon Ice

This wonderfully refreshing ice is excellent tucked inside hollow lemon shells cut zig-zag style, or served with small scoops of raspberry sorbet and vanilla bean ice cream. Guests exclaim, "Wow—this is to die for," when they taste this one.

INGREDIENTS

4 teaspoons grated lemon
   zest

$7/8$ cup sugar

$1\frac{1}{2}$ cups water

$3/4$ cup fresh lemon juice

Mash the lemon zest with 1 teaspoon of the sugar to release its oils. Combine the remaining sugar and the water in a medium saucepan and bring to a boil, stirring to dissolve the sugar. Cook until the syrup is clear. Remove from heat and stir in the lemon zest and juice. Let cool. Cover and refrigerate for 1 to 2 hours, or until thoroughly chilled.

Freeze the mixture in an ice cream maker according to the manufacturer's instructions. Or, to freeze without an ice cream maker: Pour the mixture into an 8- or 9-inch square metal pan or a half-gallon plastic container. Cover with aluminum foil, plastic wrap, or a plastic lid, and freeze until firm, about 2 to 3 hours. Transfer the mixture to an electric mixer or a food processor and beat until light and fluffy. Transfer to a container, cover, and freeze until firm, about 1 to 2 hours.

MAKES ABOUT 1 QUART

Cranberry Orange Ice

Perfect for a Thanksgiving feast, this tangy ice can serve as a dessert or as a piquant palate refresher between courses. For other occasions, add it to a menu featuring wild game, venison, or duck.

❧

INGREDIENTS

$\frac{3}{4}$ cup sugar

1 cup fresh orange juice

2 $\frac{3}{4}$ cups cranberry juice cocktail or cranapple juice

2 teaspoons grated orange zest

2 tablespoons fresh lemon juice

In a medium saucepan, combine the sugar and orange juice, and cook over medium heat until the sugar dissolves. Stir in the cranberry juice cocktail or cranapple juice, orange zest, and lemon juice. Let cool and refrigerate for 1 to 2 hours, or until thoroughly chilled.

Freeze the mixture in an ice cream maker according to the manufacturer's instructions. Or, to freeze without an ice cream maker: Pour the mixture into an 8- or 9-inch square metal pan or a half-gallon plastic container. Cover with aluminum foil, plastic wrap, or a lid, and freeze just until firm, about 2 to 3 hours. Transfer to an electric mixer or food processor and beat until light and fluffy. Turn into a container, cover, and freeze until firm, about 1 to 2 hours.

MAKES 1 QUART

Melon Ice

A frosty fruit puree makes an attractive ice, especially when mounded in a melon ring.
Consider pairing a pale green melon with an orange-hued ice, or a rosy
pink melon with a green-toned ice. Garnish with a pretty blossom.

INGREDIENTS

4 ½ cups diced honeydew,
   crenshaw, or watermelon

⅓ cup sugar

3 tablespoons fresh lime
   juice

Puree the melon in a blender or food processor. You should have 3 cups of puree. In a medium bowl, combine the puree with the sugar and lime juice and stir until dissolved. Pour into an 8- or 9-inch square metal pan or a half-gallon plastic container. Cover with aluminum foil, plastic wrap, or a lid, and freeze until firm, about 2 to 3 hours.

Transfer the mixture to an electric mixer or food processor and beat until light and fluffy. Transfer to a container, cover, and freeze until firm, about 1 to 2 hours.

MAKES ABOUT 1 QUART

Kiwi Fruit Sorbet

The crisp black seeds of kiwi fruit lend interest to this emerald green sorbet. Squeeze a lime wedge over the sorbet at serving time for added sparkle, or serve with a wedge of sugared angel food cake after a bountiful meal.

Mash the lime or lemon zest with 1 teaspoon of the sugar to release its oil. In a medium saucepan, combine the remaining sugar and the water, bring to a boil while stirring, and cook until the syrup is clear. Remove from heat, let cool, cover, and refrigerate for 1 to 2 hours, or until thoroughly chilled. In a blender or food processor, puree the kiwi fruit with the lime or lemon juice; stir in the chilled syrup.

Freeze the mixture in an ice cream maker according to the manufacturer's instructions. Or, to freeze without an ice cream maker: Pour the prepared mixture into an 8- or 9-inch square pan or a half-gallon plastic container. Cover with aluminum foil, plastic wrap, or a lid, and freeze until firm, about 2 to 3 hours. Transfer to an electric mixer or food processor and beat until light and fluffy. Transfer to a container, cover, and freeze until firm, about 1 to 2 hours. Serve with a lime wedge to squeeze over.

MAKES ABOUT 1 QUART

INGREDIENTS

2 teaspoons grated lime or lemon zest

$^3/_4$ cup sugar

$^3/_4$ cup water

8 kiwi fruit, peeled and quartered

6 tablespoons fresh lime or lemon juice

Lime wedges for garnish

Nectarine-Almond Sorbet

Flecks of red peel color this creamy gold sorbet like confetti.
After touring the sites of Ephesus, Turkey, on a sultry day, an ambrosial fresh
peach ice was served to us from an ice cart at the end of the ruins.
When I developed this recipe, nectarine proved even more wonderful.

INGREDIENTS

1 tablespoon grated lemon
zest

3/4 cup sugar

3/4 cup water

5 nectarines (about 1 1/2
pounds), pitted and sliced

2 tablespoons fresh lemon
juice

1/4 teaspoon almond
extract

Mash the lemon zest with 1 teaspoon of the sugar to release its oil. In a medium saucepan, combine the remaining sugar and the water, bring to a boil while stirring, and cook until the syrup is clear. Let cool, cover, and refrigerate for 1 to 2 hours, or until thoroughly chilled. In a blender or food processor, puree the nectarines and lemon juice; blend in the syrup and almond extract.

Freeze the mixture in an ice cream maker according to the manufacturer's instructions. Or, to freeze without an ice cream maker: Pour the prepared mixture into an 8- or 9-inch square metal pan or a half-gallon plastic container. Cover with aluminum foil, plastic wrap, or a lid, and freeze until firm, about 2 to 3 hours. Transfer to an electric mixer or food processor and beat until light and fluffy. Transfer to a container, cover, and freeze until firm, about 1 to 2 hours.

MAKES ABOUT 1 QUART

Blood Orange Sorbet

This brilliant ruby-colored ice was so delectable, it inspired me to plant a blood orange tree in the garden. Leave the pulp in the juice to add texture.

❧

INGREDIENTS

1 tablespoon grated blood
orange zest

$3/_4$ cup sugar

3 cups fresh blood orange
juice

$1/_4$ cup fresh lemon juice

Mash the blood orange zest with 1 teaspoon of the sugar to release its oil. Stir the remaining sugar into the blood orange juice and let stand until dissolved; stir in the orange zest and lemon juice. Refrigerate until thoroughly chilled, about 1 to 2 hours.

Freeze the mixture in an ice cream maker according to the manufacturer's instructions. Or, to freeze without an ice cream maker: Pour the mixture into an 8- or 9-inch square metal pan or a half-gallon plastic container. Cover with aluminum foil, plastic wrap, or a lid, and freeze until firm, about 2 to 3 hours. Transfer to an electric mixer or food processor and beat until light and fluffy. Transfer to a container, cover, and freeze until firm, about 1 to 2 hours.

MAKES ABOUT 1 QUART

Raspberry and Grand Marnier Sorbet

*A touch of orange liqueur accents this elegant raspberry sorbet. Pair it with orange gelato,
lemon ice, or vanilla bean or hazelnut ice cream. Or serve it with a medley of fresh
strawberries and raspberries. It was at Tivoli in Copenhagen that I discovered the joy
of pairing raspberry syrup with vanilla ice cream in a just-baked oversize waffle cone.
This recipe comes from friends Tita and John Kolozsi, who grow exquisite
tiny-seeded raspberries and freeze some to enjoy this delight year-round.*

In a blender or food processor, puree the raspberries. Push the puree through a sieve into a large bowl; discard the seeds. Add the orange juice, lemon juice, and sugar, stirring until the sugar is dissolved. Cover and refrigerate for 1 to 2 hours, or until thoroughly chilled.

Freeze the mixture in an ice cream maker according to the manufacturer's instructions. When the sorbet is almost completely frozen, blend in the liqueur, if desired. Or, to freeze without an ice cream maker: Pour the mixture into an 8- or 9-inch square metal pan or a half-gallon plastic container. Cover with aluminum foil, plastic wrap, or a lid, and freeze until firm, about 2 to 3 hours. Transfer to an electric mixer or food processor, and beat until light and fluffy. Blend in the liqueur, if desired. Transfer to a container, cover, and freeze until firm, about 1 to 2 hours.

MAKES 1 QUART

INGREDIENTS

4 cups fresh raspberries

1 cup fresh orange juice

$^1/_3$ cup fresh lemon juice

$1^1/_4$ cups sugar

$^1/_4$ cup Grand Marnier or
Cointreau (optional)

Very Berry Sorbet

A combination of strawberries and raspberries results in a brilliant rosy-hued sorbet,
especially pleasing served in balloon-shaped wineglasses with a few berries for garnish.
It is also divine paired with lemon ice or vanilla bean ice cream for contrast.

❧

INGREDIENTS

$3/_4$ cup sugar

$3/_4$ cup water

3 tablespoons fresh lemon
juice

$1 1/_4$ cups fresh raspberries

$2 1/_2$ cups (1 pound) fresh
strawberries, hulled

2 tablespoons framboise
liqueur (optional)

MAKES 1 QUART

In a medium saucepan, combine the sugar and water, bring to a boil while stirring, and cook until the syrup is clear. Stir in the lemon juice. Let cool, cover, and refrigerate for 1 to 2 hours, or until thoroughly chilled. In a blender or food processor, puree the raspberries and push the puree through a sieve into a large bowl; discard the seeds. Puree the strawberries, stir the puree into the raspberry puree, and stir in the chilled syrup. Refrigerate for 1 hour, or until thoroughly chilled.

Freeze the mixture in an ice cream maker according to the manufacturer's directions. When the sorbet is almost completely frozen, blend in the framboise, if desired. Or, to freeze without an ice cream maker: Pour the mixture into an 8- or 9-inch square metal pan or a half-gallon plastic container. Cover with aluminum foil, plastic wrap, or a lid. Place in the freezer and freeze until firm, about 2 to 3 hours. Transfer to an electric mixer or food processor and beat until light and fluffy. Blend in the framboise, if desired. Transfer to a container, cover, and freeze until firm, about 1 to 2 hours.

Pear-Champagne Sorbet

Choose flavorful ripe pears such as Anjou or Bosc for this delicate sorbet. It is delightful after a dinner featuring roast duck, pork tenderloin, or grilled sausages.

In a large saucepan, combine the pears, wine, sugar, nutmeg, and lemon juice and simmer until the pears are soft, about 10 minutes. Let cool, cover, and refrigerate for 1 to 2 hours, or until thoroughly chilled. Stir in the cream.

Freeze in an ice cream maker according to the manufacturer's instructions. When the mixture is almost competely frozen, blend in the brandy, if desired.

MAKES ABOUT 1 QUART

INGREDIENTS

4 large pears (about 1½ pounds), peeled, cored, and sliced

2 cups sparkling wine, Champagne, or fruity white wine, such as Riesling, Semillon, or Chenin Blanc

¾ cup sugar

¼ teaspoon freshly grated nutmeg

1 tablespoon fresh lemon juice

½ cup heavy (whipping) cream

2 to 3 tablespoons pear brandy (optional)

Espresso Granita

*Italian coffee ice provides a cool refreshment for a summer day. Top it
with brandy and whipped cream for an authentic touch.*

❧

INGREDIENTS

²/₃ cup sugar

³/₄ cup water

2 cups freshly brewed
   espresso or triple-
   strength coffee

Brandy for serving
   (optional)

Whipped cream (optional)

In a medium saucepan, combine the sugar and water,
bring to a boil while stirring, and cook until the syrup is
clear. Remove from heat, stir in the espresso or coffee,
and let cool to room temperature. Pour into an 8- or 9-
inch square metal pan or a half-gallon plastic container.
Cover with aluminum foil, plastic wrap, or a lid, and
freeze until firm, about 2 to 3 hours.

Transfer to an electric mixer or food processor and
beat until light and fluffy. Transfer to a container, cover,
and freeze until firm, about 1 to 2 hours. To serve, spoon
the granita into wineglasses. If desired, pour a teaspoon
of brandy over each serving and top with whipped cream.

MAKES ABOUT 1 QUART

Daiquiri Granita

Tuck an edible flower blossom or petals on top of this cool sweet. Nasturtium, violet, or borage blossoms, or a lavender sprig or rose petals are nice.

≈

INGREDIENTS

1 tablespoon grated lime
  zest

½ cup sugar

2 ½ cups water

⅓ cup fresh lime juice

⅓ cup dark rum

Fresh blossoms or mint
  sprigs for garnish

Mash the lime zest with ½ teaspoon of the sugar to release its oil. In a medium saucepan, combine the remaining sugar and the water, bring to a boil while stirring, and cook until the syrup is clear. Remove from the heat and stir in the lime juice, rum, and zest. Let cool, cover, and refrigerate for 1 to 2 hours, or until thoroughly chilled.

Freeze the mixture in an ice cream maker according to the manufacturer's instructions. Or, to freeze without an ice cream maker: Pour the mixture into an 8- or 9-inch square metal pan or a half-gallon plastic container. Cover with aluminum foil, plastic wrap, or a lid, and freeze until firm, about 2 to 3 hours. Transfer to an electric mixer or food processor and beat until light and fluffy. Transfer to a container, cover, and freeze until firm, about 1 to 2 hours. Serve garnished with blossoms or mint.

MAKES ABOUT 1 QUART

Strawberry Frozen Yogurt

This bright rosy-red frozen yogurt has an intense berry flavor that is wonderfully refreshing. Use a whole-milk yogurt for the best texture.

꙳

In a blender or food processor, puree the strawberries, sugar, corn syrup, and lemon juice. Turn into a large bowl and let stand for 20 minutes for the sugar to dissolve. Blend in the yogurt. Cover and refrigerate for 1 to 2 hours, or until thoroughly chilled.

Freeze the mixture in an ice cream maker according to the manufacturer's instructions. Or, to freeze without an ice cream maker: Pour the mixture into an 8- or 9-inch square metal pan or a half-gallon plastic container. Cover with aluminum foil, plastic wrap, or a lid, and freeze until firm, about 2 to 3 hours. Transfer to an electric mixer or food processor and beat until light and fluffy. Transfer to a container, cover, and freeze until firm, about 1 to 2 hours.

MAKES 1 QUART

INGREDIENTS

2 $\frac{1}{2}$ cups (1 pound) strawberries, hulled

$\frac{1}{2}$ cup sugar

$\frac{1}{4}$ cup light corn syrup

1 tablespoon fresh lemon juice

2 cups plain yogurt

Mango Tango Frozen Yogurt

*Juicy sweet mangoes mingle with banana and orange in this healthy sweet.
Use a whole-milk yogurt for the best texture. Prefreezing bananas keeps them
from darkening and allows the mixture to be made immediately.*

In a food processor or blender, combine all the ingredients and puree. Freeze in an ice cream maker according to the manufacturer's instructions. Or, to freeze without an ice cream maker: Pour the mixture into an 8- or 9-inch square metal pan or a half-gallon plastic container. Cover with aluminum foil, plastic wrap, or a lid, and freeze until firm, about 2 to 3 hours. Transfer to an electric mixer or food processor, and beat or process until light and fluffy. Transfer to a container, cover, and freeze until firm, about 1 to 2 hours.

MAKES ABOUT 1 QUART

INGREDIENTS

1 banana, peeled, frozen, and cut into $\frac{1}{2}$-inch chunks

2 navel oranges, peeled and quartered

2 large mangoes, diced (2 cups)

6 tablespoons honey or to taste

1 cup plain yogurt

Ice Creams and Gelatos

ICE CREAM IS MADE WITH A COOKED CUSTARD base blended with heavy cream to create a smooth and satiny texture. The custard is easily made a day or two in advance and refrigerated, ready for churning. The Italian version of ice cream, gelato, ranges from light to rich. These are lower in fat because they contain only a small amount of heavy cream and no egg yolks.

Vanilla Bean Ice Cream

Gianduia Ice Cream

Dark Chocolate Ice Cream

Praline Ice Cream

Coffee Bean Ice Cream with
   Bittersweet Fudge Sauce

Toasted Almond Ice Cream

Mocha-Almond Fudge
   Ice Cream

Hazelnut Ice Cream

Pistachio Ice Cream

Caramel-Pecan Ice Cream

Caramel Swirl Ice Cream

Peach Ice Cream

Candied Ginger Ice Cream

Coconut Ice Cream

Three-Fruit Ice Cream

Strawberry Ice Cream

Honey Ice Cream

Mint-Chocolate Swirl
   Ice Cream

Rum Raisin Ice Cream

Peppermint Candy Ice Cream

Quick Ice Cream Flavors

Orange Gelato

Mango Gelato

Strawberry Gelato

Apple-Calvados Gelato

Vanilla Bean Ice Cream

Flecks of vanilla bean imbue this creamy ice cream with an exotic flavor that is far superior to vanilla extract. Let the pod steep in the cream as it cools to further enhance the spicy taste. Vanilla ice cream is ideal as a topping for berry and other fruit pies, cobblers, and streusels, or mingle scoops with Raspberry, Very Berry, or Lemon Sorbet.

❧

INGREDIENTS

One 4-inch vanilla bean, halved lengthwise

2 cups half-and-half

²/₃ cup sugar

6 egg yolks, beaten

1 cup heavy (whipping) cream

Scrape the black seeds from the vanilla bean into a double boiler. Add the vanilla pods and half-and-half, and cook over barely simmering water until scalded. Whisk the sugar into the egg yolks. Whisk in some of the hot half-and-half, return this mixture to the pan, and cook over barely simmering water, stirring constantly, until the custard coats the spoon. Immediately place the pan in a pan of cold water and stir to cool to room temperature. Stir in the cream. Cover and refrigerate for 2 to 3 hours, or until thoroughly chilled.

When you are ready to freeze the mixture, remove the vanilla pods. Freeze in an ice cream maker according to the manufacturer's instructions.

MAKES 1 QUART

Gianduia Ice Cream

I first discovered this gelato at the Perchè No? and Vivoli gelaterie in Florence. There this gelato was divine. Now Bravo Fono at the Stanford Shopping Center, Palo Alto, indulges fans with their dark and rich gianduia. My friends Paulette and Lazlo Fono, the owners, researched their recipe in Italy and shared with me their secret of combining bittersweet chocolate and cocoa. Pair gianduia with coffee bean ice cream for a great duo.

※

INGREDIENTS

²/₃ cup hazelnuts

2 cups half-and-half

²/₃ cup sugar

¹/₃ cup unsweetened Dutch-
process cocoa

5 egg yolks, beaten

5 ounces bittersweet
chocolate, chopped

1 cup heavy (whipping)
cream

1 teaspoon vanilla extract

MAKES 1 GENEROUS QUART

Preheat the oven to 325°F. Place the nuts in a baking pan and bake for 10 minutes, or until lightly toasted. Turn the nuts out onto a cloth towel, wrap up, and rub them together to remove their papery skins. Let cool.

In a blender or food processor, grind the nuts until they are finely ground and start to release their oil but still have some texture.

In a double boiler, combine the nuts and 1¾ cups of the half-and-half, and heat over barely simmering water until scalded. Mix the sugar, cocoa, and remaining ¼ cup half-and-half and stir into the egg yolks. Whisk in some of the hot half-and-half mixture, return this mixture to the pan, and cook over barely simmering water, stirring constantly, until the custard coats the spoon. Stir the chocolate into the custard until the chocolate melts. Immediately place the pan in a pan of cold water and stir to cool to room temperature.

Stir the cream and vanilla into the mixture. Cover and refrigerate for 2 to 3 hours, or until thoroughly chilled. Freeze in an ice cream maker according to the manufacturer's instructions.

46

Dark Chocolate Ice Cream

A top-quality bittersweet chocolate lends an intense flavor to this ice cream.

Ingredients

6 ounces bittersweet
chocolate, chopped

2 cups half-and-half

²/₃ cup sugar

5 egg yolks, beaten

1 cup heavy (whipping)
cream

1 teaspoon vanilla extract

In a double boiler, heat the half-and-half over barely simmering water until scalded. Whisk the sugar into the egg yolks. Whisk in some of the hot half-and-half, return the mixture to the pan, and cook over barely simmering water, stirring constantly, until the custard coats the spoon. Stir the chocolate into the custard until the chocolate melts. Immediately place in a pan of cold water, and stir to cool to room temperature.

Stir the cream and vanilla into the mixture. Cover and refrigerate for 2 to 3 hours, or until thoroughly chilled. Freeze in an ice cream maker according to the manufacturer's instructions.

Makes 1 quart

48

Praline Ice Cream

Years ago in Scandinavia I discovered ice cream cones dipped in almond praline or grated chocolate. This was a custom of the ice cream carts that dotted the many pretty parks throughout Norway and Sweden. After a noontime picnic of reindeer meat, cardamom buns, and pears, a candy-coated cone was a sought-after finale. Crunchy caramel candy laces this ice cream for a seductive pairing with sliced fresh peaches, pineapple chunks, or strawberries.

To MAKE THE PRALINE: Butter a sheet of aluminum foil. In a small, heavy saucepan, combine the sugar and water and cook over medium heat, shaking the pan, until the sugar caramelizes and turns a light amber color. (Note: If the caramel should crystallize, cover the pan with a lid to wash down the sugar crystals.) Add the nuts and shake to coat them with syrup. Turn out onto the buttered aluminum foil and let cool. Finely chop the praline or place it in a blender or food processor and blend until fine.

In a double boiler, heat the half-and-half over barely simmering water until scalded. Whisk the sugar into the egg yolks. Whisk in some of the hot half-and-half, return this mixture to the pan, and cook over barely simmering water, stirring constantly, until the custard coats the spoon. Immediately place the pan in a pan of cold water, and stir to cool to room temperature.

Stir the cream and vanilla into the mixture. Cover and refrigerate for 2 to 3 hours, or until thoroughly chilled. Freeze in an ice cream maker according to the manufacturer's instructions. When partially frozen, mix in the praline.

INGREDIENTS

Praline
$\frac{1}{2}$ cup sugar
2 tablespoons water
$\frac{1}{2}$ cup chopped almonds

2 cups half-and-half
$\frac{2}{3}$ cup sugar
5 egg yolks, beaten
1 cup heavy (whipping) cream
1 teaspoon vanilla extract

MAKES 1 QUART

Coffee Bean Ice Cream with Bittersweet Fudge Sauce

*Whole coffee beans are steeped in cream to make this deeply flavored ice cream.
Choose a coffee with an aroma you like. A Mocha-Java or Ethiopian Harrar bean is
my preference. As a shortcut you can substitute coffee granules for the beans.*

❧

INGREDIENTS

6 tablespoons coffee beans,
   or 3 tablespoons freeze-
   dried coffee granules
2 cups half-and-half
²/₃ cup sugar
6 egg yolks, beaten
1 cup heavy (whipping)
   cream

Bittersweet Fudge Sauce
6 ounces bittersweet
   chocolate, chopped
¹/₂ cup half-and-half
¹/₄ cup light corn syrup
¹/₂ teaspoon vanilla extract

In a double boiler, combine the coffee beans and half-and-half. Heat over barely simmering water for 30 to 40 minutes, or until the coffee flavor is pronounced to your liking. Whisk the sugar into the egg yolks. Whisk in some of the hot half-and-half mixture, return this mixture to the pan, and cook over barely simmering water, stirring constantly, until the custard coats the spoon. Immediately place the pan in a pan of cold water and stir to cool to room temperature.

Strain the custard base into a container and discard the beans. Stir in the cream. Cover and refrigerate for 2 to 3 hours, or until thoroughly chilled. Freeze in an ice cream maker according to the manufacturer's instructions.

TO MAKE THE FUDGE SAUCE: Combine the chocolate pieces, half-and-half, and corn syrup in the double boiler. Cook over barely simmering water, stirring, until the mixture is smooth. Stir in the vanilla. Serve warm in a pitcher and pour over the ice cream at the table.

MAKES 1 QUART

Toasted Almond Ice Cream

Crisp almonds stud this ice cream, which is delectable served with fresh sliced peaches, nectarines, raspberries, or blueberries. If you like, drizzle the ice cream with a little Amaretto.

Preheat the oven to 325°F. Place the nuts in a baking pan and bake for 10 minutes, or until lightly toasted. Let cool and finely chop.

In a double boiler, heat the half-and-half over barely simmering water until scalded. Whisk the sugar into the egg yolks. Whisk in some of the hot half-and-half, return this mixture to the pan, and cook over barely simmering water, stirring constantly, until the custard coats the spoon. Immediately place the pan in a pan of cold water and stir to cool to room temperature.

Stir the cream and vanilla into the mixture. Cover and refrigerate for 2 to 3 hours, or until thoroughly chilled. Freeze in an ice cream maker according to the manufacturer's instructions. When partially frozen, mix in the nuts.

MAKES 1 QUART

INGREDIENTS

$^1/_2$ cup natural, shelled almonds

2 cups half-and-half

$^2/_3$ cup sugar

5 egg yolks, beaten

1 cup heavy (whipping) cream

1 teaspoon vanilla extract

Mocha-Almond Fudge Ice Cream

A swirl of chocolate fudge and toasted almonds embellishes this coffee-flavored ice cream.

Preheat the oven to 325°F. Place the nuts in a baking pan and bake for 10 minutes, or until toasted. Set aside.

In a double boiler, combine the coffee beans and half-and-half, and cook over hot water for 30 to 40 minutes, or until the coffee flavor is pronounced to your liking. Whisk the sugar into the egg yolks. Whisk in some of the hot half-and-half mixture, return this mixture to the pan, and cook over barely simmering water, stirring constantly, until the custard coats the spoon. Immediately place the pan in a pan of cold water and stir to cool. Strain the mixture into a container and discard the beans. Stir in the cream. Cover and refrigerate for 2 or 3 hours, or until thoroughly chilled.

Meanwhile, prepare the chocolate fudge: In a small saucepan, combine the sugar and cocoa. Stir in the half-and-half and corn syrup. Stirring constantly, cook over medium heat until the mixture comes to a boil. Simmer for 2 minutes and stir in the butter and vanilla. Let cool.

Freeze the mixture in an ice cream maker according to the manufacturer's instructions. When partially frozen, mix in the toasted almonds. When almost completely frozen, swirl in the chocolate fudge using a rubber spatula.

MAKES 1 QUART

INGREDIENTS

1/2 cup almonds, chopped

6 tablespoons coffee beans

2 cups half-and-half

2/3 cup sugar

5 egg yolks, beaten

1 cup heavy (whipping) cream

Chocolate Fudge

2 tablespoons sugar

2 tablespoons unsweetened Dutch process cocoa

2 tablespoons half-and-half

1/4 cup light corn syrup

1 tablespoon unsalted butter

1/4 teaspoon vanilla extract

Hazelnut Ice Cream

Called nocciola *in Italy and* noisette *in France, hazelnut gelato,* glace, *or ice cream is a beloved flavor of mine. I love to pair it with small scoopfuls of Raspberry and Grand Marnier Sorbet or Very Berry Sorbet. Ground nuts permeate the base of this ice cream, lending an intriguing texture. It is essential to grind the nuts to the point that they release their oil. Scent the ice cream with a little Frangelico, the hazelnut liqueur, if you wish.*

❧

INGREDIENTS

¹/₂ cup hazelnuts

2 cups half-and-half

²/₃ cup sugar

6 egg yolks, beaten

1 cup heavy (whipping) cream

1 tablespoon Frangelico, or ¹/₂ teaspoon vanilla extract

Preheat the oven to 325°F. Place the nuts in a baking pan and bake for 10 minutes, or until lightly toasted. Turn the nuts out onto a cloth towel, wrap up, and rub them together to remove their papery skins. Let cool.

In a blender or food processor, grind the nuts until they are very finely ground and start to release their oil but still have texture. In a double boiler, combine the nuts and half-and-half. Cook over barely simmering water for 15 minutes. Whisk the sugar into the egg yolks. Whisk in some of the hot half-and-half mixture, return this mixture to the pan, and cook over barely simmering water, stirring constantly, until the custard coats the spoon. Immediately place the pan in a pan of cold water and stir to cool.

Stir the cream and Frangelico or vanilla into the mixture. Cover and refrigerate for 2 to 3 hours, or until thoroughly chilled. Freeze in an ice cream maker according to the manufacturer's instructions. When partially frozen, mix in the nuts.

MAKES 1 QUART

Pistachio Ice Cream

Both fine flecks and butter-browned caramelized chunks of pistachios lace this pale green ice cream. It makes a lovely adjunct to a Moroccan or Middle Eastern dinner.

꙳

INGREDIENTS

1 cup pistachios

2 cups half-and-half

²/₃ cup plus 2 teaspoons sugar

4 egg yolks, beaten

1 teaspoon unsalted butter

1 cup heavy (whipping) cream

1 teaspoon vanilla extract

In a blender or food processor, blend ⅔ cup of the nuts until finely ground. In a double boiler, combine the nuts and half-and-half. Cook over barely simmering water for 15 minutes. Whisk the ⅔ cup sugar into the egg yolks. Whisk in some of the hot half-and-half mixture, return this mixture to the pan, and cook over barely simmering water, stirring constantly, until the custard coats the spoon. Immediately place the pan in a pan of cold water and stir to cool. Stir in the cream and vanilla. Cover and refrigerate for 2 to 3 hours, or until thoroughly chilled.

In a small skillet, melt the butter and the remaining 2 teaspoons sugar over medium heat. Coarsely chop the remaining ⅓ cup pistachios and sauté them until lightly browned; let cool.

Freeze the mixture in an ice cream maker according the manufacturer's instructions. When partially frozen, mix in the sugared nuts, or sprinkle them over the ice cream at serving time.

MAKES 1 QUART

Caramel-Pecan Ice Cream

*Burnt sugar ice cream with toasted pecans is a wonderful complement to a peach,
apple, or pear tart or an autumn fruit cobbler or upside-down cake.
Or serve a scoop on gingerbread or dessert waffles.*

In a heavy saucepan, combine the sugar and 1/4 cup of the water. Cook over medium heat, shaking the pan, until the sugar melts and caramelizes to a light amber color. Be careful, as the syrup is very hot. (If the sugar should crystallize before melting, put a lid on the pan to wash down the sugar crystals on the sides, rather than stirring the mixture.) Carefully pour in the remaining 1/4 cup water—it will steam and bubble. Carefully add the half-and-half and cook, stirring, until the syrup remelts. Whisk some of the hot half-and-half mixture into the egg yolks.

Pour the mixture into a double boiler and cook over barely simmering water, stirring constantly, until the custard coats the spoon. Immediately place the pan in a pan of cold water and stir to cool. Stir in the cream and vanilla. Cover and refrigerate for 2 to 3 hours, or until thoroughly chilled.

In a saucepan, melt the butter over medium heat and sauté the nuts until golden brown; let cool.

Freeze the mixture in an ice cream maker according to the manufacturer's instructions. When partially frozen, mix in the nuts.

INGREDIENTS

3/4 cup sugar

1/2 cup water

1 1/2 cups half-and-half

6 egg yolks, beaten

1 1/2 cups heavy (whipping)
   cream

1 teaspoon vanilla extract

2 teaspoons unsalted butter

1/2 cup pecans, walnuts, or
   Brazil nuts, chopped

MAKES 1 QUART

Caramel Swirl Ice Cream

Caramel laces this ice cream with chewy candy for a delicious topping on an open-face pear tart or an apple crisp.

⚜

Ingredients

2 cups half-and-half

²/₃ cup sugar

6 egg yolks, beaten

1 cup heavy (whipping) cream

1 tablespoon vanilla extract

Caramel Sauce

¹/₂ cup sugar

¹/₄ cup half-and-half

2 tablespoons unsalted butter

1 tablespoon light corn syrup

1 teaspoon unsalted butter (optional)

¹/₂ cup Brazil nuts or pecans, chopped (optional)

Makes 1 quart

In a double boiler, heat the half-and-half over barely simmering water until scalded. Whisk the sugar into the egg yolks. Whisk in some of the hot half-and-half, return this mixture to the pan, and cook over barely simmering water, stirring constantly, until the custard coats the spoon. Immediately place the pan in a pan of cold water and stir to cool to room temperature. Stir in the cream and vanilla. Cover and refrigerate for 2 to 3 hours, or until thoroughly chilled.

To make the caramel sauce: In a small, heavy saucepan, heat the sugar over medium heat until it melts and turns a light amber color. Carefully stir in the half-and-half, butter, and corn syrup. Cook and stir until smooth and slightly thickened, about 2 minutes. Let cool to room temperature. If using the nuts, melt the butter in a small saucepan over medium heat, add the nuts, and stir until golden; let cool.

Freeze the ice cream mixture in an ice cream maker according to the manufacturer's instructions. When partially frozen, add the nuts, if used. When almost completely frozen, swirl in the cool caramel sauce with a rubber spatula.

Peach Ice Cream

Full-flavored ripe peaches at the height of the season are a must for this ice cream. It is delicious with praline cookies, amaretti, or almond biscotti.

In a double boiler, combine the half-and-half and cream, and heat over barely simmering water until scalded. Whisk ½ cup of the sugar into the egg yolks. Whisk in some of the hot cream, return this mixture to the pan, and cook over hot water, stirring constantly, until the custard coats the spoon. Immediately place the double boiler in a pan of cold water and stir to cool to room temperature. Cover and refrigerate for 2 to 3 hours, or until thoroughly chilled.

Shortly before you wish to freeze the ice cream, peel, pit, and slice the peaches. Mash them with a potato masher or puree them in a food processor and sprinkle with the remaining ¼ cup sugar; let stand until the sugar dissolves, about 30 minutes. Stir the peach puree and vanilla into the custard base. Freeze in an ice cream maker according to the manufacturer's instructions.

MAKES 1 GENEROUS QUART

INGREDIENTS

½ cup half-and-half

1 cup heavy (whipping) cream

¾ cup sugar

3 egg yolks, beaten

4 ripe peaches (about 1 pound)

1 teaspoon vanilla extract or to taste

Candied Ginger Ice Cream

Hot, sweet bites of candied ginger spark this smooth ice cream made with fresh ginger.
The inspiration for this recipe came from a beautiful dessert sampled at the Ritz in
London: a cookie tulip holding seven sorbets, including ginger, and an array
of exotic fruits. It resembled a flower from another galaxy.

INGREDIENTS

2 cups half-and-half

$1/2$ cup chopped peeled
fresh ginger

$2/3$ cup sugar

5 egg yolks, beaten

1 cup heavy (whipping)
cream

1 teaspoon vanilla extract

$1/3$ cup candied ginger,
chopped

In a double boiler, combine the half-and-half and fresh ginger and heat over barely simmering water until scalded. Set aside and let steep for 15 minutes. Whisk the sugar into the egg yolks. Whisk in some of the hot half-and-half mixture, return this mixture to the pan, and cook over barely simmering water, stirring constantly, until the custard coats the spoon. Immediately place the pan in a pan of cold water and stir to cool to room temperature. Push through a sieve, discarding the ginger fibers. Stir in the cream and vanilla.

Cover and refrigerate the mixture for 2 to 3 hours, or until thoroughly chilled. Freeze in an ice cream maker according to the manufacturer's instructions. When partially frozen, mix in the candied ginger.

MAKES 1 QUART

Coconut Ice Cream

Reminiscent of the tropics, this ice cream is lovely paired with pineapple ice or mango gelato. Or, serve it with hot fudge sauce. Canned coconut milk is available in a light version that works well here.

In a blender or food processor, blend the coconut until finely shredded. In a double boiler, combine the coconut and coconut milk, and heat over barely simmering water for 15 minutes. Whisk the sugar into the egg yolks. Whisk in some of the hot coconut milk mixture, return this mixture to the pan, and cook over barely simmering water, stirring constantly, until the custard coats the spoon. Immediately place the pan in a pan of cold water and stir to cool to room temperature.

Stir the cream and vanilla into the mixture. Cover and refrigerate for 2 to 3 hours, or until thoroughly chilled. Freeze in an ice cream maker according to the manufacturer's instructions.

MAKES 1 QUART

INGREDIENTS

$^3/_4$ cup flaked coconut

One 14-ounce can light coconut milk

$^1/_2$ cup sugar

4 egg yolks, beaten

1 $^1/_4$ cups heavy (whipping) cream

$^1/_2$ teaspoon vanilla extract

Three-Fruit Ice Cream

As delicious today as it was decades ago, this old-fashioned combination was a childhood favorite of mine. It begs for a slice of ripe banana or fresh pineapple alongside.

❧

INGREDIENTS

2 cups half-and-half

²/₃ cup sugar

6 egg yolks, beaten

1 cup heavy (whipping)
   cream

1 banana

³/₄ cup orange juice

3 tablespoons fresh
   lemon juice

1 tablespoon grated orange
   zest (optional)

In a double boiler, heat the half-and-half over barely simmering water until scalded. Whisk the sugar into the egg yolks. Whisk in some of the hot half-and-half, return this mixture to the pan, and cook over barely simmering water, stirring constantly, until the custard coats the spoon. Immediately place the pan in a pan of cold water and stir to cool to room temperature. Blend in the cream. Cover and refrigerate the mixture for 2 to 3 hours, or until thoroughly chilled.

When you are ready to freeze the ice cream mixture, puree the banana, orange juice, and lemon juice in a blender or food processor until smooth. Stir into the custard base with the orange zest, if used. Freeze in an ice cream maker according to the manufacturer's instructions.

MAKES 1 GENEROUS QUART

Strawberry Ice Cream

This luscious berry ice cream is one of the best of its kind. It is sublime alone or with a crisp sugar cooky or butter wafer for contrast. A classic flavor, it conjures memories of Fourth of July picnics long ago.

In a double boiler, combine the half-and-half and cream, and heat over barely simmering water until scalded. Whisk the sugar into the egg yolks. Whisk in some of the hot cream, return to the pan, and cook over barely simmering water, stirring constantly, until the custard coats the spoon. Immediately place the pan in a pan of cold water, and stir to cool to room temperature. Cover and refrigerate for 2 to 3 hours, or until thoroughly chilled.

About 30 minutes before you wish to freeze the ice cream, puree the berries in a blender or food processor, sprinkle with the remaining sugar, and let stand until the sugar dissolves. Stir the berry puree into the custard base. Freeze in an ice cream maker according to the manufacturer's instructions.

MAKES 1 GENEROUS QUART

INGREDIENTS

$\frac{1}{2}$ cup half-and-half

1 cup heavy (whipping) cream

$\frac{3}{4}$ cup sugar

3 egg yolks, beaten

2 $\frac{1}{2}$ cups (1 pound) fresh strawberries, hulled

Honey Ice Cream

*Honey and orange zest scent an ice cream flavored with anise or licorice liqueur,
pleasant counterpoints to the honey sweetness. The idea for this recipe comes from a
licorice glace served with caramelized pear slices at L'Espérance in Burgundy. This is also
lovely topped with fresh blueberries or a medley of raspberries and strawberries.*

In a double boiler, heat the half-and-half over barely simmering water until scalded. Whisk the honey into the egg yolks. Whisk in some of the hot half-and-half, return this mixture to the pan, and cook over barely simmering water, stirring constantly, until the custard coats the spoon. Immediately place the pan in a pan of cold water and stir to cool to room temperature. Stir in the cream.

Cover and refrigerate the mixture for 2 to 3 hours, or until thoroughly chilled. Freeze in an ice cream maker according to the manufacturer's instructions. When the ice cream is almost frozen, mix in the liqueur.

MAKES 1 QUART

Variation: Omit the Sambuca, Pernod, or Galliano. Add 1 tablespoon orange zest to the egg yolks and mix in 2 tablespoons Cointreau when the ice cream is almost completely frozen.

INGREDIENTS

$1\frac{1}{2}$ cups half-and-half

$\frac{2}{3}$ cup orange blossom honey or another fragrant honey

6 egg yolks, beaten

$1\frac{1}{2}$ cups heavy (whipping) cream

2 tablespoons Sambuca, Pernod, or Galliano

Mint-Chocolate Swirl Ice Cream

Fine quality, old-fashioned natural peppermints, like the American Mint brand, add a cool counterpoint to the chocolate ribbons that thread this sumptuous ice cream.

❧

INGREDIENTS

1 cup (4 ounces) natural (uncolored) peppermint candies

2 cups half-and-half

5 egg yolks, beaten

1 cup heavy (whipping) cream

1 teaspoon vanilla extract

Chocolate Swirl

4 ounces bittersweet chocolate, chopped

$\frac{1}{3}$ cup half-and-half

$\frac{1}{4}$ cup light corn syrup

$\frac{1}{4}$ teaspoon vanilla extract

In a double boiler, combine the candies and half-and-half, and heat over barely simmering water until scalded; set aside and let steep for 15 minutes, or until the candies are melted. Whisk some of the hot half-and-half mixture into the egg yolks, return this mixture to the pan, and cook over hot water, stirring constantly, until the custard coats the spoon. Immediately place the pan in a pan of cold water, and stir to cool to room temperature. Stir in the cream and vanilla. Cover and refrigerate for 2 to 3 hours, or until thoroughly chilled.

Meanwhile, prepare the chocolate swirl: In a double boiler, combine the chocolate, half-and-half, and corn syrup. Heat over barely simmering water, stirring, until smoothly blended. Stir in the vanilla. Let cool.

Freeze the ice cream mixture in an ice cream maker according to the manufacturer's instructions. When the ice cream is almost completely frozen, blend in the chocolate swirl using a rubber spatula.

MAKES 1 QUART

Rum Raisin Ice Cream

Golden raisins plumped in rum are suspended in this creamy ice cream. Try a scoop as the topping for a caramel or brown sugar streusel cake or an apple pie.

✴

Place the raisins in a small bowl and pour the rum over; let steep for 15 minutes. In a double boiler, heat the half-and-half over barely simmering water until scalded. Whisk the sugar into the egg yolks. Whisk in some of the hot half-and-half, return this mixture to the pan, and cook over barely simmering water, stirring constantly, until the custard coats the spoon.

Drain the raisins, reserving the rum, and stir them into the custard. Immediately place the pan in a pan of cold water and stir to cool to room temperature. Stir the cream and vanilla into the mixture. Cover and refrigerate for 2 to 3 hours, or until thoroughly chilled. Freeze in an ice cream maker according to the manufacturer's instructions. When almost completely frozen, blend in the remaining rum.

MAKES 1 QUART

INGREDIENTS

3/4 cup golden raisins

1/4 cup dark rum

2 cups half-and-half

2/3 cup sugar

5 egg yolks, beaten

1 cup heavy (whipping) cream

1/2 teaspoon vanilla extract

Peppermint Candy Ice Cream

*This pale pink ice cream is colored naturally by the candy, so the number
of egg yolks has been decreased slightly to keep the color pure.
When I was a child, this was a holiday treat made with a 1-inch-thick stick of
peppermint candy, and a great mate to the chocolate Christmas log.*

ༀ

INGREDIENTS

1 3/4 cups (7 ounces) striped
  peppermint candies or
  candy cane
2 cups half-and-half
3 egg yolks, beaten
1 cup heavy (whipping)
  cream
1 teaspoon vanilla extract

In a double boiler, combine 1¼ cups of the candy
with the half-and-half and heat over barely simmering
water until scalded; set aside and let steep for 15 minutes,
or until the candy is melted. Whisk some of the hot half-
and-half mixture into the egg yolks, return this mixture
to the pan, and cook over barely simmering water, stirring
constantly, until the custard coats the spoon. Immediately place the pan in a pan of cold water and stir to cool
to room temperature.

Stir the cream and vanilla into the mixture. Cover
and refrigerate until thoroughly chilled. Freeze in an
ice cream maker according to the manufacturer's instructions. When almost completely frozen, mix in the
remaining candy.

MAKES 1 QUART

Quick Ice Cream Flavors

Biscotti Cookie Bar Ice Cream: Finely chop two 2-ounce Biscotti Cookie Bars (Joseph Schmidt dark chocolate with a La Tempesta almond biscotti flavor) and blend them into 1 quart vanilla or coffee ice cream when the ice cream is almost frozen. Freeze for 2 hours, or until firm.

Almond Toffee Ice Cream: Finely chop ounces 4 ounces almond toffee or Almond Roca candy. Blend into 1 quart vanilla ice cream when the ice cream is almost frozen. Freeze for 2 hours, or until firm.

Butterfinger Crunch Ice Cream: Chop two 2.6-ounce Butterfinger bars into small pieces. Blend into 1 quart vanilla or coffee ice cream when the ice cream is almost frozen. Freeze for 2 hours, or until firm.

Candied Chestnut Ice Cream: Drain one 8-ounce jar whole chestnuts in syrup, reserving the syrup. Chop the chestnuts into pieces the size of hazelnuts. Blend into 1 quart vanilla ice cream when the ice cream is almost frozen. Freeze for 2 hours, or until firm. Heat the reserved chestnut syrup with 2 tablespoons Cognac and serve scoops of ice cream with the warm syrup poured over.

Cookie Crumb Ice Cream: Finely crush 8 to 10 Hydrox or Oreo cookies to make 1 cup large crumbs. Blend into 1 quart vanilla, coffee, or chocolate ice cream when the ice cream is almost frozen. Freeze for 2 hours, or until firm.

Orange Gelato

Fresh orange juice exudes its sun-sweet tang in this light gelato. Cream gives it just a touch of richness. Partner with a slice of double-chocolate cake or a chocolate waffle.

≈

Mash the orange zest with 1 teaspoon of the sugar to release its oil. Combine the remaining sugar and the water in a medium saucepan, bring to a boil while stirring, and cook until the syrup is clear. Remove from heat and stir in the orange juice, lemon juice, and orange zest. Let cool, cover, and refrigerate for 1 to 2 hours, or until thoroughly chilled. Stir in the cream.

Freeze the mixture in an ice cream maker according to the manufacturer's instructions.

MAKES 1 QUART

INGREDIENTS

1 tablespoon grated orange zest

$^2/_3$ cup sugar

$^2/_3$ cup water

2 cups fresh orange juice

$^1/_4$ cup fresh lemon juice

$^2/_3$ cup heavy (whipping) cream

Mango Gelato

This looks festive served in glass bowls with a pretty blossom, such as a nasturtium,
violet, or calendula, tucked on top. Let it follow a salad luncheon or a Moroccan or
Asian dinner menu featuring duck or grilled pork or chicken kabobs.

INGREDIENTS

½ cup sugar

½ cup water

2 large mangoes (about
  1 ¾ pounds), peeled,
  cut from the pit, and
  diced

⅓ cup fresh lime juice

⅔ cup heavy (whipping)
  cream

In a medium saucepan, combine the sugar and water, bring to a boil while stirring, and cook until the syrup is clear. Remove from the heat and let cool to room temperature. Puree the diced mangoes in a blender or food processor with the lime juice and syrup. Cover and refrigerate for 1 to 2 hours, or until thoroughly chilled. Stir in the cream.

Freeze the mixture in an ice cream maker according to the manufacturer's instructions.

MAKES ABOUT 1 QUART

Strawberry Gelato

This pretty pink gelato is great for a children's birthday party. Serve it in small cups.

In a blender or a food processor, puree the berries with 2 tablespoons of the sugar. In a medium saucepan, combine the remaining sugar and the water, bring to a boil while stirring, and cook until the syrup is clear. Remove from the heat and let cool to room temperature; stir in the berry puree and lemon juice. Cover and refrigerate for 1 to 2 hours, or until thoroughly chilled. Stir in the cream.

Freeze the mixture in an ice cream maker according to the manufacturer's instructions.

MAKES ABOUT 1 QUART

INGREDIENTS

4 cups (about 1 1/2 pounds) fresh strawberries, hulled

2/3 cup sugar

2/3 cup water

3 tablespoons fresh lemon juice

2/3 cup heavy (whipping) cream

Apple-Calvados Gelato

Surprisingly easy to make, this is a refreshing mate to apple pie or baked apples.

In a large bowl, stir the apple juice and sugar together and let stand until the sugar is dissolved. Stir in the milk and cream. Cover and refrigerate for 1 to 2 hours, or until thoroughly chilled.

Freeze the mixture in an ice cream maker according to the manufacturer's instructions. Blend in the Calvados or Cognac, if desired, when almost completely frozen. Or, to freeze without an ice cream maker: Pour the prepared mixture into an 8- or 9-inch square metal pan or a half-gallon plastic container. Cover with aluminum foil, plastic wrap, or a lid, and freeze until firm, about 2 to 3 hours. Transfer to an electric mixer or food processor and beat until light and fluffy. Blend in the Calvados or Cognac. Transfer to a container, cover, and freeze until firm, about 1 to 2 hours.

MAKES 1 GENEROUS QUART

INGREDIENTS

1 cup apple juice

$3/_4$ cup sugar

1 cup milk

$3/_4$ cup heavy (whipping) cream

2 tablespoons Calvados or Cognac (optional)

Frozen Mousses, Parfaits, and Bombes

A MOLDED FROZEN DESSERT IS IDEAL make-ahead fare for a party. These can be done several days in advance. Molds such as brioche pans, tall cylindrical pans, and square pans make decorative shapes. Frozen mousses, parfaits, and bombes are festive presentations for a dinner with company.

Frozen Chocolate Amaretti Mousse

*This rich chocolate dessert was a discovery at the one-star Hiély-Lucullus
on the rue République in Avignon, France, years ago. The frozen confection has
long been a favorite of mine for party entertaining.*

❦

INGREDIENTS

1 ¼ cups sugar

⅓ cup water

1 teaspoon light corn syrup

4 egg whites

8 ounces bittersweet
chocolate, chopped

½ cup freshly brewed
double-strength coffee

1 teaspoon vanilla extract

1 ½ cups heavy (whipping)
cream

¼ cup dark rum, Kahlúa,
or Cointreau

12 amaretti cookies

MAKES 12 SERVINGS

In a small saucepan, combine the sugar, water, and corn syrup and bring to a boil. Boil over high heat until the temperature reaches 238°F on a candy thermometer, or until a small amount dropped into a glass of cold water forms a soft, pliable ball. Meanwhile, in an electric mixer, beat the egg whites until soft peaks form. Gradually beat the hot syrup into the egg whites. Continue beating the mixture until it cools to room temperature, about 7 minutes.

Combine the chocolate and coffee in a double boiler and heat over barely simmering water until melted, stirring to blend. Let cool. Stir the vanilla into the chocolate mixture. Fold a third of the egg white mixture into the chocolate to lighten it, then fold this mixture into the remaining egg whites. In a deep bowl, whip the cream until soft peaks form. Stir in 2 tablespoons of the rum or liqueur and fold into the chocolate mixture.

Spoon the mousse into a 9- or 10-inch springform pan. Dip the cookies in the remaining 2 tablespoons liqueur and arrange on top. Cover and freeze until firm. To serve, remove the pan sides, place the frozen mousse on a platter, and cut into wedges.

White Chocolate Parfait

Freeze this silken parfait ahead, ready to top with raspberries or blueberries or to sprinkle with pistachios or toasted almonds at serving time.

In a double boiler, beat the egg yolks and sugar until thick and pale in color. Whisk in the milk. Place over barely simmering water and whisk until tripled in volume. Remove from heat and stir in the white chocolate until melted. Immediately place the pan in a pan of cold water and stir to cool to room temperature

In a deep bowl, whip the cream until soft peaks form. Fold the vanilla into the cream, then fold the cream mixture into the white chocolate mixture. Spoon into individual soufflé dishes or small dessert bowls, cover, and freeze until firm. To serve, top with berries or nuts, if desired.

MAKES 6 SERVINGS

INGREDIENTS

6 egg yolks

$^1/_2$ cup sugar

1 cup milk

6 ounces white chocolate, chopped, or white chocolate chips

1 cup heavy (whipping) cream

1 teaspoon vanilla extract

Fresh raspberries, blueberries, or pistachios, or toasted almonds for garnish (optional)

Pistachio Paradiso

This frothy egg yolk, sugar syrup, and whipped cream mixture is the basis of many semifreddo flavors. It is also shaped into many famous Italian ice cream molds, such as St. Honore and zuccotto. Molded in a decorative fluted or square mold, it makes a decorative party dessert.

❧

INGREDIENTS

Candied Pistachios

1 teaspoon butter

2 tablespoons sugar

$1/2$ cup pistachios, coarsely
   chopped

$3/4$ cup sugar

$1/4$ cup water

4 egg yolks

$1^1/_4$ cups heavy (whipping)
   cream

$1/2$ teaspoon vanilla extract

2 tablespoons Sambuca,
   Pernod or other favorite
   anise- or licorice-flavored
   liqueur

About 3 cups fresh
   raspberries or straw-
   berries for garnish
   (optional)

To make the candied nuts: Butter a sheet of aluminum foil. In a small skillet, melt the butter over medium heat and add the sugar. Heat for 1 minute and stir in the nuts. Cook, stirring, until the sugar melts and turns a light caramel color and the nuts are golden. Turn out of the pan onto the buttered aluminum foil and let cool; break apart.

In a small, heavy saucepan, combine the sugar and water and bring to a boil. Boil until the temperature registers 238°F on a candy thermometer, or until a small amount dropped into a glass of cold water forms a soft, pliable ball. Meanwhile, in an electric mixer, beat the egg yolks until thick and pale in color. Gradually beat in the hot syrup. Continue beating until the mixture cools to room temperature, about 7 minutes; cover and refrigerate for 2 hours, or until thoroughly chilled.

In a deep bowl, whip the cream until soft peaks form. Fold in the vanilla and liqueur. Fold the whipped cream and ½ cup of the candied pistachios into the chilled egg mixture. Turn into a 6-cup mold. Cover and freeze until firm, about 3 hours.

Unmold the dessert by dipping the mold into a pan of hot water for a few seconds, then invert the mold onto a serving platter. Return to the freezer for 20 to 30 minutes to firm up. To serve, garnish the top with the remaining candied pistachios. If desired, ring with berries.

MAKES 8 SERVINGS

Grand Marnier Semifreddo

A sugar syrup beaten into egg yolks creates an especially airy, mousselike dessert.
At Bologna's celebrated restaurant Diana, goblets of this semifreddo arrive
at tableside topped with warm chocolate sauce.

❧

INGREDIENTS

²/₃ cup plus 1 teaspoon
    sugar

1 tablespoon light corn
    syrup

¹/₄ cup water

4 egg yolks

2 teaspoons grated orange
    zest

2 cups half-and-half

1 cup heavy (whipping)
    cream

3 tablespoons Grand
    Marnier

In a small saucepan, combine the ²/₃ cup sugar, the corn syrup, and water and bring to a boil. Boil until the temperature reaches 238°F on a candy thermometer, or until a small amount dropped into a glass of cold water forms a soft, pliable ball. Meanwhile, in an electric mixer, beat the egg yolks until thick and pale in color; pour the sugar syrup over them in a fine stream. Continue beating until the mixture cools to room temperature, about 7 minutes. Cover and refrigerate for 2 hours, or until thoroughly chilled.

Mash the orange zest with 1 teaspoon sugar to release the oil and stir into the mousse mixture with the half-and-half and cream. Freeze in an ice cream maker according to the manufacturer's instructions. When almost completely frozen, blend in the Grand Marnier.

MAKES 1 QUART

Bombe Capriccio

Beautiful ice cream bombes in various shapes grace the freezers of the Italian pastry shops. With this soft mousse filling, they are easy to duplicate at home. The Italian word capriccio means "at the whim or fancy of the cook" when used in the title of a recipe.

Pack the ice cream firmly into the bottom and sides of an 8-cup ice cream, salad, or pudding mold. Freeze until firm. In a small, heavy saucepan, combine the sugar and water. Bring to a boil over medium heat and boil until the temperature registers 238°F on a candy thermometer, or until a small amount dropped into a glass of cold water forms a soft, pliable ball.

Meanwhile, beat the egg yolks with an electric mixer until thick and pale in color. Pour the sugar syrup over the egg yolks in a fine stream while beating, and continue beating until the mixture cools to room temperature, about 7 minutes. Cover and refrigerate for 2 hours, or until thoroughly chilled.

In a deep bowl, whip the cream until soft peaks form. Stir in the rum or liqueur and fold the cream mixture into the mousse mixture. Fold in ½ cup of the praline and spoon into the center of the ice cream–lined mold, filling to the top. Cover and freeze until firm, about 3 hours.

To unmold, dip the mold in a pan of hot water for a few seconds, then invert the mold on a serving platter. Sprinkle with the reserved praline. Cut in wedges to serve.

INGREDIENTS

1 quart coffee ice cream, slightly softened

¾ cup sugar

¼ cup water

4 egg yolks, beaten

1½ cups heavy (whipping) cream

2 tablespoons dark rum or a favorite liqueur such as Cointreau or Amaretto

⅔ cup Praline (page 49)

MAKES 12 SERVINGS

Raspberry-Amaretto Bombe

Prepare this glorious bombe a couple of days or even 1 week in advance for a party.
A fluted metal mold or brioche pan makes a decorative bombe, and it is easy
to cut each scalloped flute into an individual wedge at serving time.

Preheat the oven to 325°F. Scatter the nuts in a baking pan and heat in the oven for 8 to 10 minutes, or until lightly toasted; set aside. Pack the sorbet firmly into the bottom and sides of a 10-cup ice cream, salad, or pudding mold, making a ¾-inch layer. Freeze until firm.

Sprinkle the cookie crumbs with 2 tablespoons of the liqueur, if desired. Set aside. In a deep bowl, whip the cream until stiff peaks form. Beat in the remaining liqueur, if desired, or the almond extract. In a large chilled bowl, whisk the ice cream until it is light and forms mounds. Quickly fold in the whipped cream, almonds, chocolate, and cookie crumbs. Turn into the sorbet-lined mold. Cover and freeze until firm, about 3 hours.

To unmold, dip the mold into hot water for a few seconds, then invert onto a serving platter. Ring with berries. Cut into wedges to serve.

MAKES 12 SERVINGS

INGREDIENTS

½ cup blanched almonds

1 quart raspberry or strawberry sorbet

8 amaretti, crumbled

4 tablespoons Amaretto liqueur (optional)

1 cup heavy (whipping) cream

¼ teaspoon almond extract (omit if using liqueur)

1½ pints vanilla ice cream, slightly softened

1½ ounces bittersweet chocolate, coarsely grated

Fresh strawberries or raspberries for garnish

Index

M

Mango Gelato, 78

Mango Tango Frozen Yogurt, 41

Melon Ice, 24

Mint-Chocolate Swirl Ice Cream, 70

Mocha-Almond Fudge Ice Cream, 53

N

Nectarine-Almond Sorbet, 28

O

Orange Gelato, 77

P

Peach Ice Cream, 61

Pear-Champagne Sorbet, 35

Peppermint Candy Ice Cream, 72

Pistachio Ice Cream, 56

Pistachio Paradiso, 89

Praline Ice Cream, 49

R

Raspberry-Amaretto Bombe, 93

Raspberry and Grand Marnier Sorbet, 31

Rum Raisin Ice Cream, 71

S

Strawberry Frozen Yogurt, 39

Strawberry Gelato, 79

Strawberry Ice Cream, 67

T

Three-Fruit Ice Cream, 64

Toasted Almond Ice Cream, 51

V

Vanilla Bean Ice Cream, 44

Very Berry Sorbet, 32

W

White Chocolate Parfait, 87

Table of Equivalents

The exact equivalents in the following tables have been rounded for convenience.

US/UK

oz=ounce

lb=pound

in=inch

ft=foot

tbl=tablespoon

fl oz=fluid ounce

qt=quart

Metric

g=gram

kg=kilogram

mm=millimeter

cm=centimeter

ml=milliliter

l=liter

Weights

US/UK	Metric
1 oz	30 g
2 oz	60 g
3 oz	90 g
4 oz (¼ lb)	125 g
5 oz (⅓ lb)	155 g
6 oz	185 g
7 oz	220 g
8 oz (½ lb)	250 g
10 oz	315 g
12 oz (I lb)	375 g
14 oz	440 g
16 oz (1 lb)	500 g
1½ lb	750 g
2 lb	1 kg
3 lb	1.5 kg

Oven Temperatures

Fahrenheit	Celsius	Gas
250	120	½
275	140	1
300	150	2
325	160	3
350	180	4
375	190	5
400	200	6
425	220	7
450	230	8
475	240	9
500	260	10